Energize Your Fingers Every Day™

Helen Marlais with Timothy Brown

DAY ONE **1** · DAY TWO **2** · DAY THREE **3** · DAY FOUR **4** · DAY FIVE **5**

★ LESSON DAY

THE FJH MUSIC COMPANY INC.

Frank J. Hackinson

Production: Frank J. Hackinson
Production Coordinators: Joyce Loke and Satish Bhakta
Cover: Terpstra Design, San Francisco
Cover and Interior Illustrations: Nina Victor Crittenden, Minneapolis, Minnesota
Text Design and Layout: Terpstra Design, Maritza Cosano Gomez, and Andi Whitmer
Engraving: Tempo Music Press, Inc.
Printer: Tempo Music Press, Inc.

ISBN-13: 978-1-56939-944-6

M000007566

ABOUT THE AUTHORS

Dr. Marlais is one of the most prolific authors in the field of educational piano books and an exclusive writer for The FJH Music Company Inc. The critically acclaimed and award-winning piano series, *Succeeding at the Piano*® *A Method for Everyone, Succeeding with the Masters*®, *The Festival Collection*®, *In Recital*®, *Sight Reading and Rhythm Every Day*,® *Write, Play, and Hear Your Theory Every Day*,® and *The FJH Contemporary Keyboard Editions*, among others, included in *The FJH Pianist's Curriculum*® by Helen Marlais, are designed to guide students from the beginner through advanced levels. Dr. Marlais has given pedagogical workshops in virtually every state in the country and presents showcases for FJH at the national piano teachers' conventions.

As well as being the Director of Keyboard Publications for The FJH Music Company, Dr. Marlais is also an Associate Professor of Music at Grand Valley State University in Grand Rapids, Michigan, where she teaches piano majors, directs the piano pedagogy program, and coordinates the young beginner piano program. She also maintains an active piano studio of beginner through high school age award-winning students.

Dr. Marlais has given collaborative recitals throughout the United States and in Canada, Italy, England, France, Hungary, Turkey, Germany, Lithuania, Estonia, China and Australia, and has premiered many new works by contemporary composers from the United States, Canada, and Europe. She has performed with members of the Chicago, Pittsburgh, Minnesota, Grand Rapids, Des Moines, Cedar Rapids, and Beijing National Symphony Orchestras and has recorded on Gasparo, Centaur and Audite record labels with her husband, concert clarinetist Arthur Campbell. She has also recorded numerous educational piano CD's on Stargrass Records®.

Dr. Marlais received her DM in piano performance and pedagogy from Northwestern University and her MFA in piano performance from Carnegie Mellon University. Visit: www.helenmarlais.com

Timothy Brown's music has been influenced greatly by the Italian film composer Ennio Morricone. His music is noted for its "immediate emotional impact" and its roots in the neo-romantic style of music composition. Traditional formal structural elements are embedded in his wide array of compositions which includes orchestral, ballet, choral and chamber works and a body of work specifically written for piano and pedagogical purposes. He did his undergraduate studies at Bowling Green State University and received his master's degree in piano performance from the University of North Texas. His past teachers include Adam Wodnicki, Newel Kay Brown and Robert Xavier Rodriguez. He was a recipient of a research fellowship from Royal Holloway, University of London, where he performed his postgraduate studies in music composition and orchestration with the English composer, Brian Lock. He later continued his research at the well-known Accademia Nazionale di Santa Cecilia in Rome, Italy.

His numerous credits as a composer include the first prize at the Aliénor International Harpsichord Competition for his harpsichord solo *Suite Española* (Centaur records). His works are frequently performed throughout North America and Europe, and at numerous international venues including The World Piano Pedagogy Conference, and the Festival Internacional de Música de Tecla Española in the Andalusian town of Almeria, Spain. His music has been performed by concert artists, Helen Marlais, Elaine Funaro, and Arthur Campbell. Recent programs include his original compositions showcased at the Spoleto Music Festival, and the Library of Congress Concert Series in Washington D.C.

His recent commissions and performances include world premieres by the Chapman University Chamber Orchestra and Concert Choir, the Carter Albrecht Music Foundation, the Rodgers Center for Holocaust Education, and the Daniel Pearl Music Foundation, and a commissioned work and article by the American composer, Denes Agay, for Clavier Magazine. Recent works also include a commissioned Ballet by the Dallas Ballet Foundation to write the orchestral score for the Ballet Petite, *The Happy Prince* based on a short story by Oscar Wilde. Timothy Brown is an exclusive composer/clinician for The FJH Music Company Inc.

TABLE OF CONTENTS

In this book, you will practice seven techniques. Once they become a habit, you will play with beauty, speed, and ease!

1) Good Posture:

Playing with good posture is the Number 1 way to play with a healthy, tension-free body and create an excellent sound.

Sitting at the piano, imagine a daisy is growing through your spine and out the very top of your head! The daisy is gently pulling your body up until it is tall, long, and balanced. Form a natural and rounded hand shape on the keys.

2) Arm Weight:

Using arm weight will help you to play with a beautiful sound.

How to do it:

a) Sit comfortably at the piano bench and raise your arm and hand to any key. Lift your wrist slightly above the key to prepare for a drop into the key.

b) Then, drop your wrist with the weight of your arm to the bottom of the key.

c) Roll your wrist forward and release the key.

You can remember this feeling of arm weight by calling it "Drip-Drop-Roll."

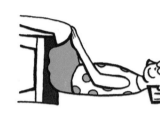

3) Flexible Wrists:

Playing with flexible wrists will help you play with easy motions, as well as help you to make beautiful musical sounds.

How to do it:

a) Rest fingers 2 and 3 gently on your thigh or on a tabletop.

b) Roll your left wrist in a clockwise motion.

c) Next, roll your right wrist in a counter-clockwise motion.

d) Notice that the hand and forearm moves along with the wrist.

When you use arm weight, along with flexible wrists, you will be able to play tension-free, which is very important.

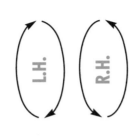

4) Strong Fingers:

Playing with strong fingers will help you to play evenly and with a beautiful tone.

It is important to play with strong fingers that do not "dent" in at the first knuckle joint.

How to do it:

a) Tap your 2nd finger on a table top or on the closed lid of the piano, using a little bit of pressure. Let your wrist be flexible and not locked. Focus on how the cushion of your fingertip makes contact with the table top/lid.

b) Tap by moving from the top knuckle that forms the strong bridge of your hand.

c) Now tap with the 3rd, then 4th, then 5th fingers in the same way.

d) When tapping with your thumb, keep in mind to play on the outside tip of your thumbnail. Never play on the full, flat side of your thumb, because this collapses the wrists and the forearms and causes tension in your fingers and underneath your wrist.

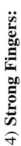

5) **Weight Transfer:**

Keep in mind that when playing, your fingers, hands, wrists, and arms should move together, at the same time, as one playing unit. Imagine a strong bridge from your shoulder to your fingertips.

Learning to transfer, or shift, your weight from one finger to the next will also help you to play with a beautiful sound. You will be able to play fast passages quickly and evenly, and slow passages with great control.

*   When you play, feel that your arm is directly behind each finger in use. Using weight transfer will allow you to play with control, ease, and agility.

6) Two-note slurs:

A mark of a fine musician is one who plays expressively. Playing two-note slurs well helps you to play musically.

mf mp

How to do it:

a) Lift your wrist slightly away from the keys. Then drop your wrist with arm weight on the first note.

b) Play the second note with a quieter sound. While you play the key, roll your hand forward onto your fingertip and then lift.

Think of the "Drip-Drop-Roll" motion and you will be able to play two-note slurs with ease!

7) Rotation:

This important technique helps you to move from one key to another without stretching or reaching. Use weight transfer in this technique to move freely from one finger to the next.

Imagine that your arms, wrists, and hands rock from side to side, the same way a boat rocks gently from side to side when it is docked in water.

The fingers, hand, wrist, and arm **move together,** at the same time, side to side.

Play with strong fingers and without dents to make this technique easy!

How to do it:

a) Lift the wrist over the key to prepare.

b) Then drop the wrist with arm weight into a key.

c) Rotate your hand, wrist, and arm in the direction of the next finger that plays.

d) The rotation gesture will be small if the interval is small, and larger if the interval is larger.

FJH2164

Unit 2

Excellent Posture Feels Good

- Stand on your tiptoes and reach for the sky!
- Then let your arms drop to your sides. Stand tall and well balanced.
- Repeat and then sit at the piano bench, feeling your excellent posture.

Up in the Morning and Ready to Go!
(flexible wrists)

* Play without "dents" in your fingers.

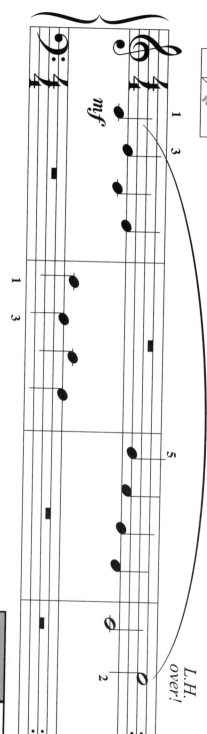

L.H. over!

No Dent!

2

Drop into each key and then bounce lightly out of each key.

Studying Studiously
(arm weight, strong fingers)

DID IT!

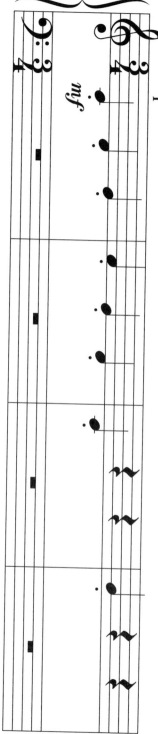

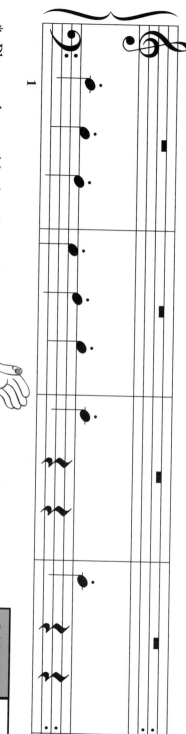

* Play on the outside tip of your thumbnails.

DID IT!

3
DAY THREE

If I Could Walk on a Cloud
(two-note slurs)

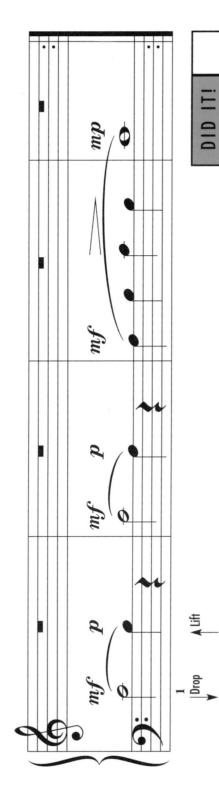

4
DAY FOUR

Falling into a Cozy Chair
(arm weight)

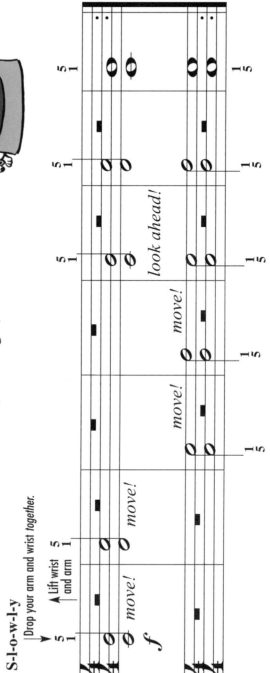

S-l-o-w-l-y

look ahead!

5 DAY FIVE

Running Up a Hill and Then Back Down
(two–note slurs)

* Listen for a louder first note in every two note slur.

(*mf mp mf mp*)   *listen!*   *mf*

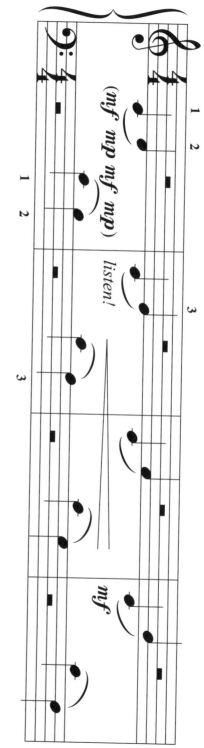

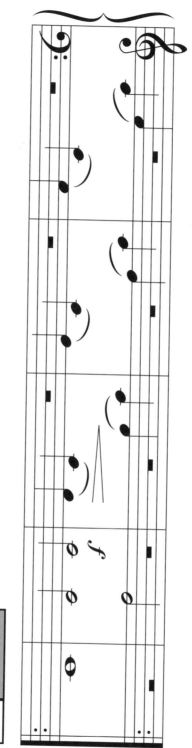

f

I Like Girls with Pig Tails
(arm weight, strong fingers)

* Play on the outside tip of your thumbnails.

DID IT!

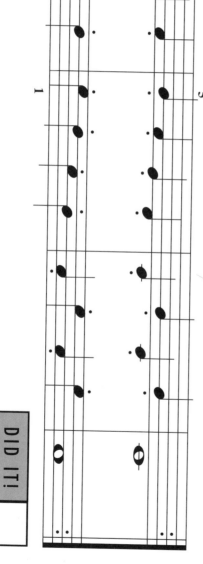

mf

DID IT!

- Play your favorite piece of the week for your teacher. Then, your teacher may have you play another one.

Teacher comments: _____

Unit 3

Excellent Posture
Makes Everything Right

- Sit quietly on the piano bench with your arms relaxed.
- Breathe in slowly…1…2…3…feel your stomach grow as you breathe in.
- Exhale slowly…1…2…3…notice how your stomach goes back to normal.

On a Seesaw at the Park
(rotation, weight transfer)

DAY ONE

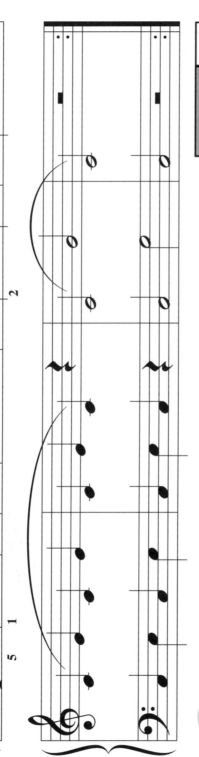

DID IT!

Walking Through Mud
(arm weight)

* Play heavily, on the **outside** tip of your thumbnails.

DAY TWO

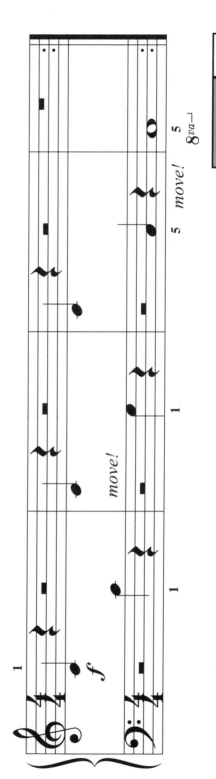

DID IT!

FJH2164

3

Peek-a-Boo
(arm weight, strong fingers)

* Keep your wrist and arm moving as "one unit" without bending your wrist.

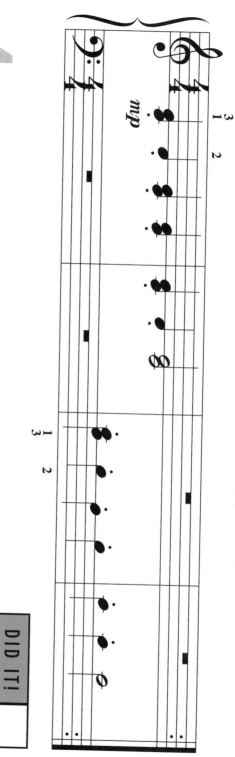

mp

4

Nodding My Head
(arm weight, flexible wrists)

* Look for a letter "C" between your thumb and second finger. This is the shape you need to see when playing.

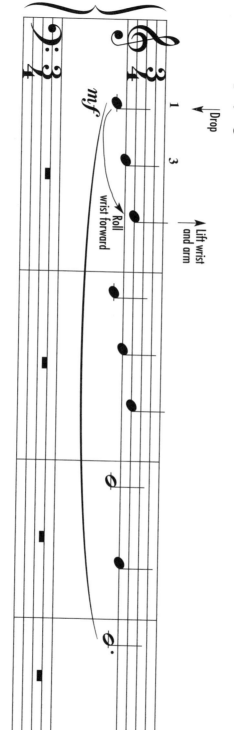

mf

Roll
wrist forward

Drop

Lift wrist
and arm

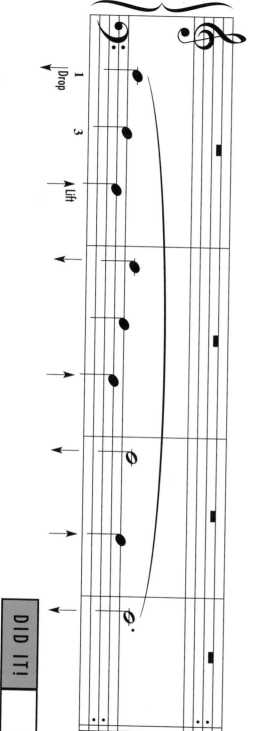

Drop

Lift

Tapping My Head with My L.H. at the Same Time I Rub My Belly with My R.H.

(weight transfer in R.H., strong fingers)

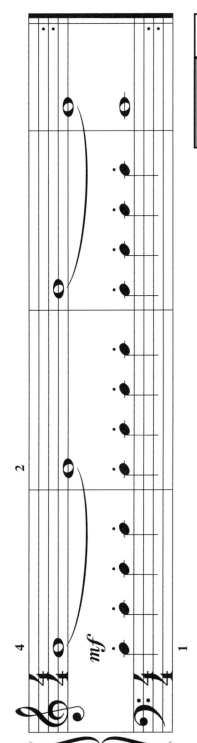

DID IT!

Tapping My Head with My R.H. at the Same Time I Rub My Belly with My L.H.

(weight transfer in L.H., strong fingers)

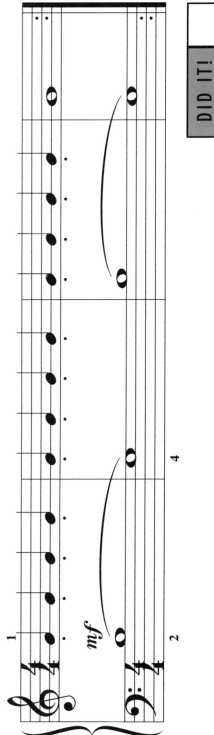

DID IT!

★ LESSON DAY

• Play your favorite piece of the week for your teacher. Then, your teacher may have you play another one.

Teacher comments: _____

Unit 4

Healthy and Flexible Playing:
Shoulder Rolls

- Roll your right shoulder slowly round and round. Do this five times.
- Roll your left shoulder slowly round and round. Do this five times.
- Now go the opposite direction! And roll the shoulders together!

Taking Small Steps
(arm weight, flexible wrists)

* On every note, drop your arm weight to the bottom of the key. Then make two slow circles with your wrists, R.H. ↻, and L.H. in the opposite direction. Call them, "two-circle round ups!"

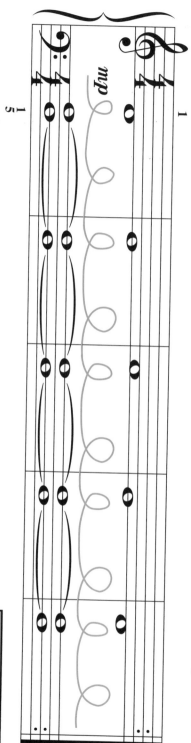

mp

1
5

DID IT!

DAY TWO

Trying to Walk with Gum
on the Bottom of My Right Shoe
(arm weight)

- Drop your arm into the keys. Notice your forearm, wrist and hand moving together.

S-l-o-w-l-y

2 1 3 1 4 1 5
          1

f

DID IT!

Trying to Walk with Gum
on the Bottom of My Left Shoe

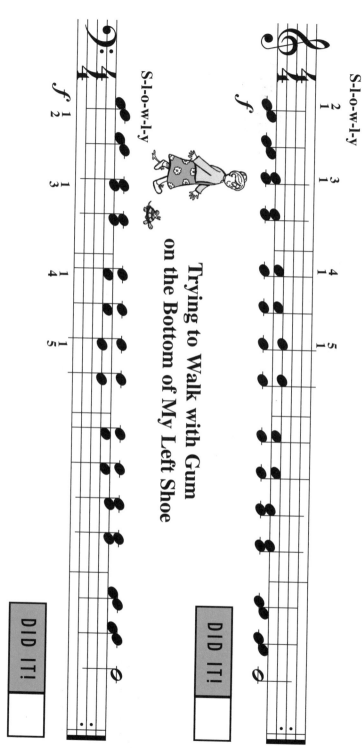

S-l-o-w-l-y

f
1 1 1 1
2 3 4 5

DID IT!

DAY THREE

The Woodpecker
(strong fingers, weight transfer)

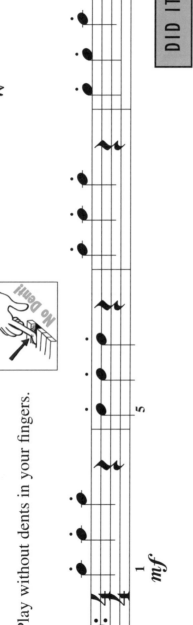

No Dent!

* Play without dents in your fingers.

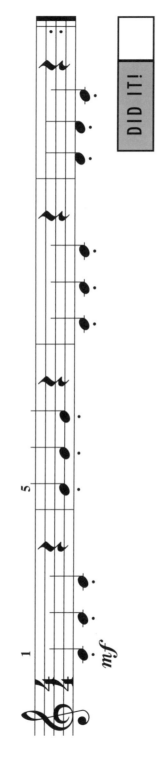

DID IT!

DID IT!

DAY FOUR

In a Big Hurry!
(two-note slurs)

Drop arm weight

Lift wrist quickly!

DID IT!

DAY FIVE

Raking Leaves in the Yard
(flexible wrists, weight transfer)

* The first time, play *staccato*. The second time, play *legato*.

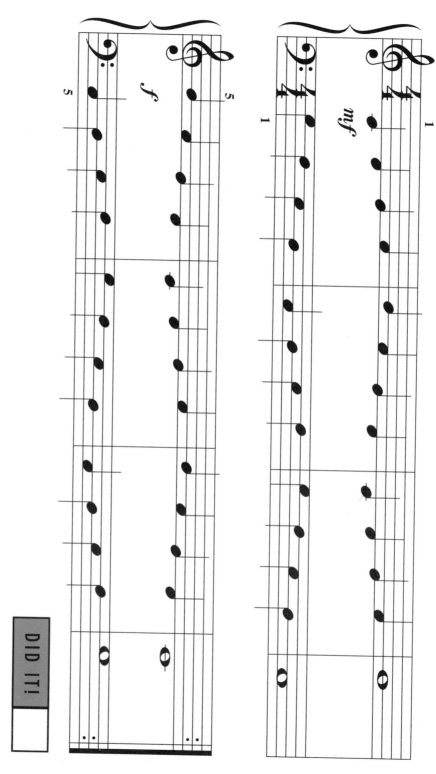

DID IT!

Making a Leaf House

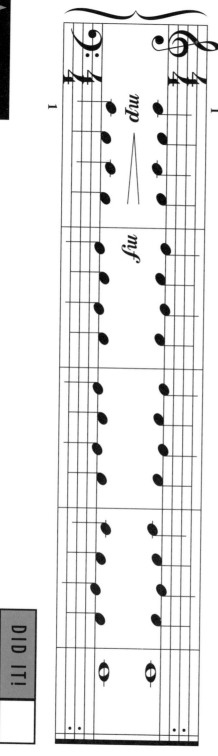

DID IT!

★ LESSON DAY

• Play your favorite piece of the week for your teacher. Then, your teacher may have you play another one.

Teacher comments: _____

Unit 5

1
D A Y O N E

Good Posture:
Getting Ready to Play!

- Sit toward the front half of the bench with your body weight evenly distributed between your feet and the seat.
- Sit far enough from the piano so that you can let your elbows and arms move freely.

Hop-A-Long
(arm weight, flexible wrists)

2nd time, play faster!

mf

L.H. over!

DID IT!

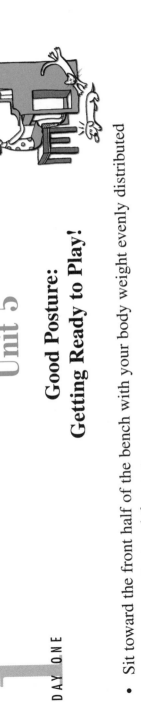

2
D A Y T W O

Warming Up in Ballet Class
(two-note slurs)

mp

Drop — Lift — Drop — Lift — Drop — Lift — Drop — Lift

DID IT!

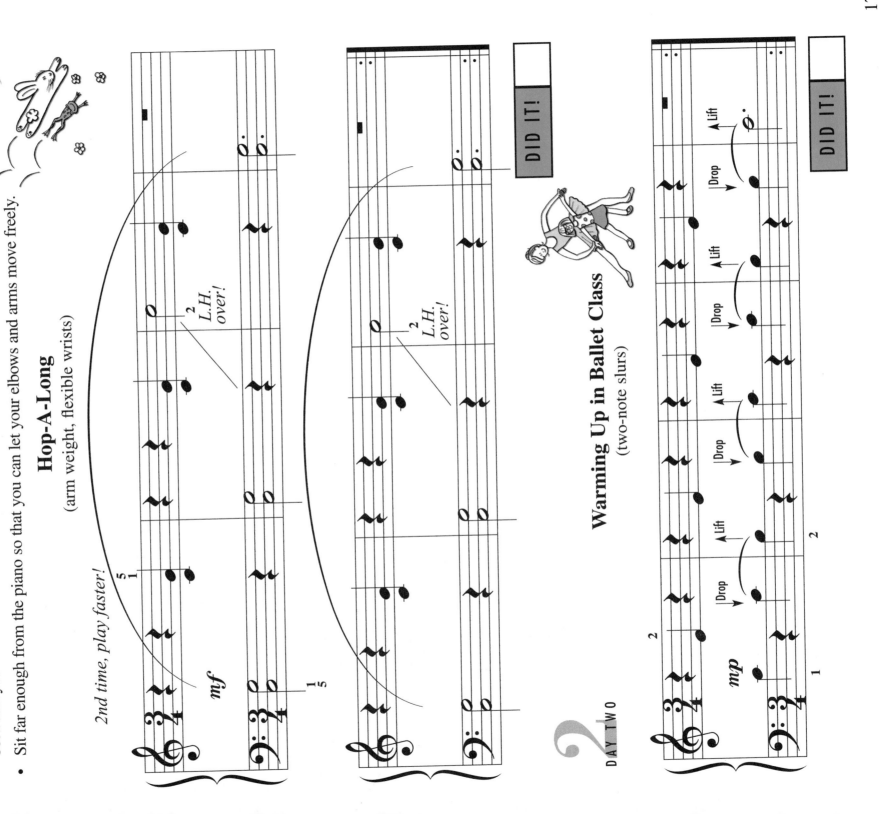

FJH2164

3

Sailing the Basketball Through the Hoop
(weight transfer, flexible wrists)

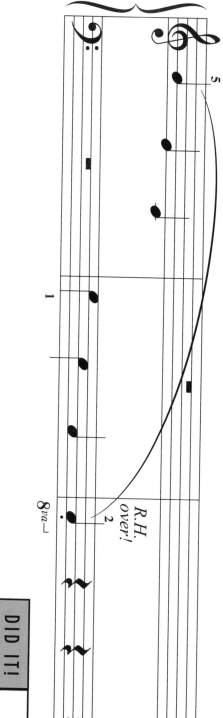

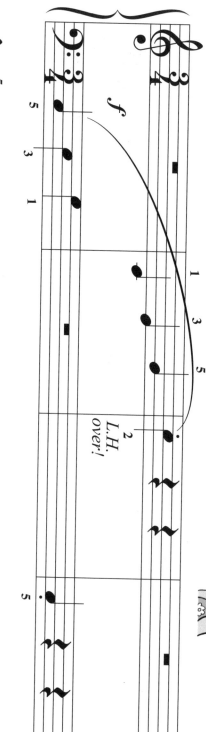

4

Bouncing a Small Ball
(weight transfer)

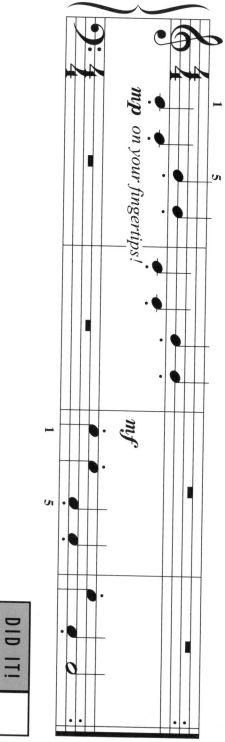

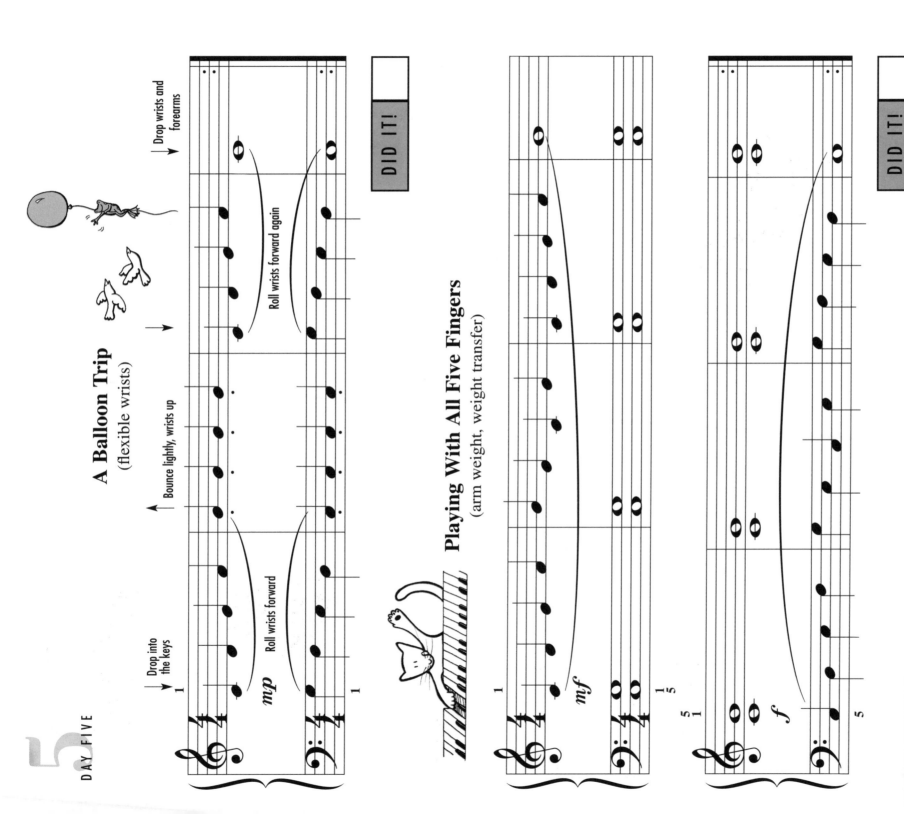

Unit 6

Feeling Good Posture:
The Elephant Trunk Warm-Up

- Stand up with your shoulders relaxed - low and wide. Bend the upper half of your body over. Look at your toes. Let your arms and head dangle in front of you.

- Clasp your hands and swing your arms from left to right, like an elephant swinging its trunk from side to side.

- Then straighten up again. Do you notice how good you feel?

Snowboarding
(arm weight, flexible wrists)

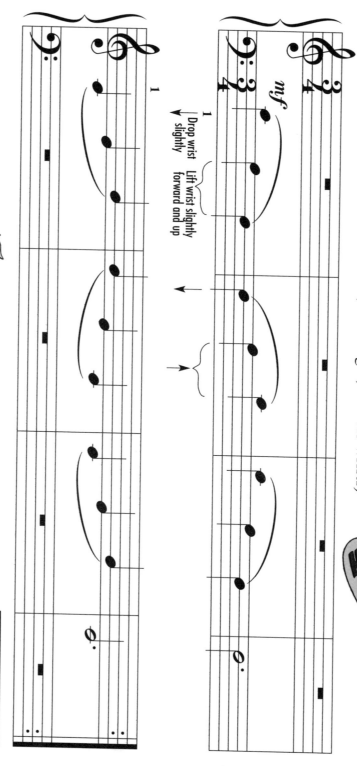

DID IT!

Reaching the Finish Line
(arm weight, flexible wrists)

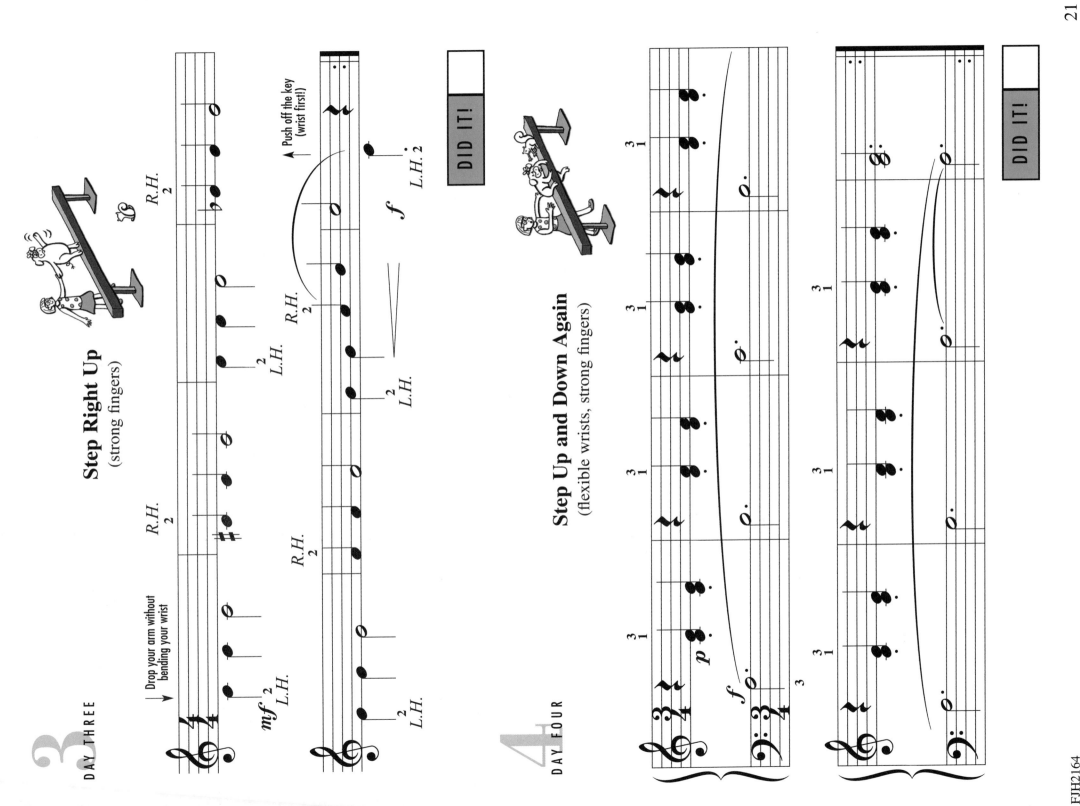

5 DAY FIVE

On the Balance Beam
(rotation)

mf *very smoothly*

f

DID IT!

On the Uneven Bars
(weight transfer, strong fingers)

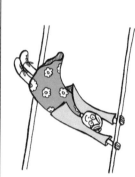

mp

mf

f

8*va* R.H. over!

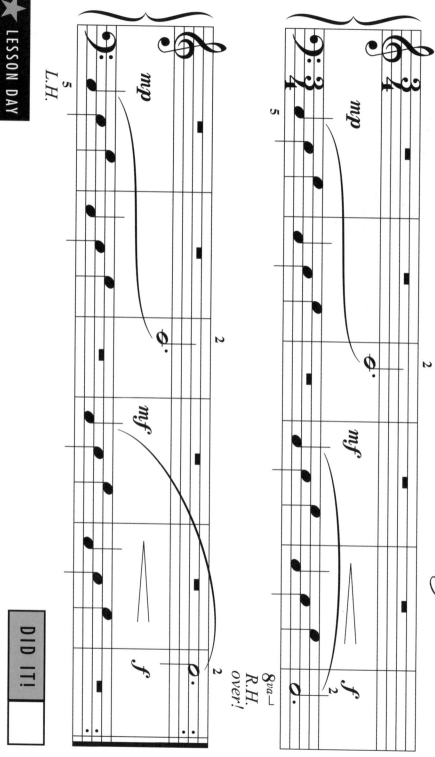

L.H.

mp

mf

f

DID IT!

• Play your favorite piece of the week for your teacher. Then, your teacher may have you play another one.

Teacher comments: _____

Unit 7

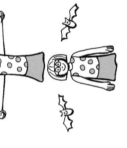

Feeling Good Posture:
The Flying Bat Warm-Up

- Stretch your arms straight out to your sides - clench your fists.
- Count 1 - 2 - 3! Hold the stretch!
- Then let your arms drop to your sides.
- Let all the tension go. Do you notice how good you feel?
- You are ready to make music today!

Kite in the Air
(rotation in the R.H.)

L.H. legato if you can!

DID IT!

Eating Meatballs
(rotation in the L.H.)

DID IT!

3

New Position:

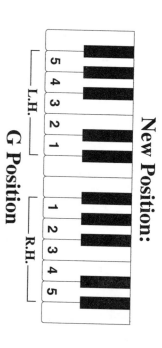

L.H. — 5 4 3 2 1

R.H. — 1 2 3 4 5

G Position

Dinosaur Walk
(arm weight)

* Drop forearm and wrist at the same time.

1
1
2
1
3
1
4
1

f

even louder!

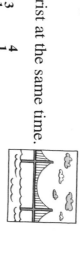

DID IT!

4
DAY FOUR

Another Dinosaur
(arm weight)

f
1
2
1
3
1
4
1

even louder!

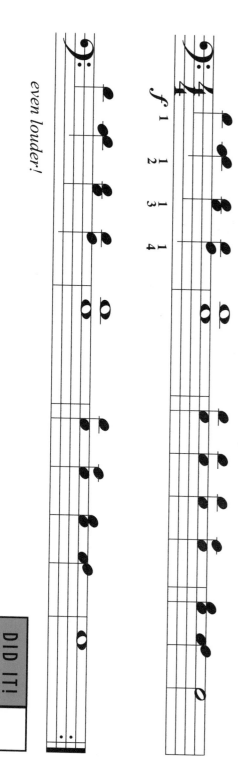

DID IT!

DAY FIVE

Playing Leap Frog
(two–note slurs, flexible wrists)

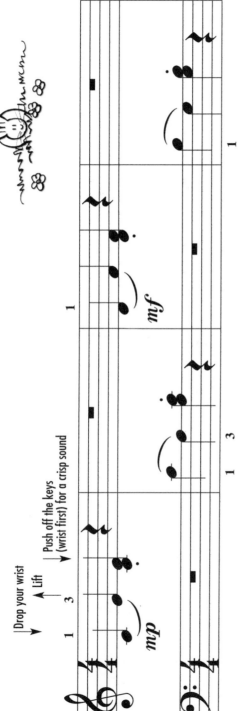

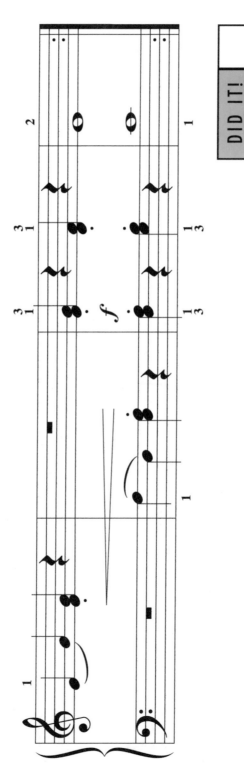

DID IT!

 **LESSON DAY**

- Play your favorite piece of the week for your teacher. Then, your teacher may have you play another one.

Teacher comments: _____

Unit 8

Excellent Posture:
The Shrugging Monkey

DAY ONE

- Press your shoulders to your ears.
- Hold it!
- Then let your shoulders drop low and wide.
- Do this three more times.
- Notice how good it feels to release the tension in your shoulders.
- You are ready to make music today!

Carrying Heavy Bricks on a Hot Day
(arm weight, rotation in the R.H.)

S-l-o-w-l-y

DID IT!

DAY TWO

The Giant is Coming
(arm weight, strong fingers)

DID IT!

3 DAY THREE

Hammering a Small Nail in the Wall
(strong fingers)

TAP TAP TAP

mf

mf

DID IT!

4 DAY FOUR

Through the Rainbow
(two-note slurs)

R.H.   *R.H.*   *R.H.*

L.H. 2   *L.H. 2*   *L.H. 2*

Drop ▲Lift

Drop ▲Lift

mf

DID IT!

DAY FIVE

Peaches Are Sweet
(flexible wrists, weight transfer)

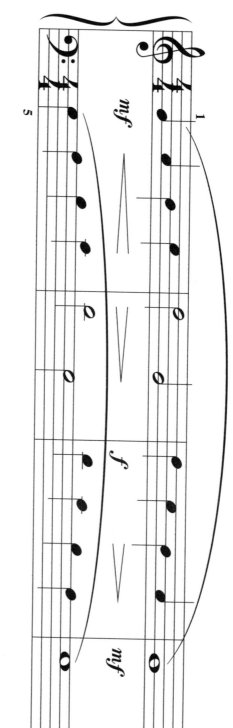
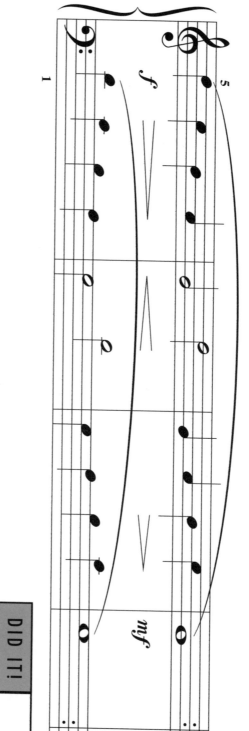

DID IT!

★ **LESSON DAY**

• Play your favorite piece of the week for your teacher. Then, your teacher may have you play another one.

Teacher comments: _____

Unit 9

DAY ONE

Healthy Playing:
Skimming the Keys

- Sitting on the piano bench, lean slightly forward into the keyboard with your upper torso.

- Now lean to your right, and pretend to play the high notes by swirling your arm in a blowing windy motion.

- Then lean to your left, and pretend to play the low notes the same way.

- Do you feel balanced on your hip bones?

On a Surf Board
(flexible wrists, weight transfer)

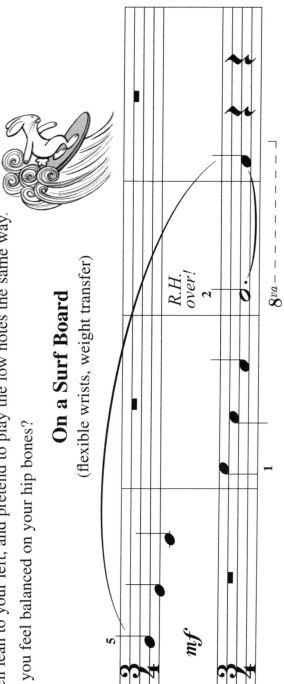

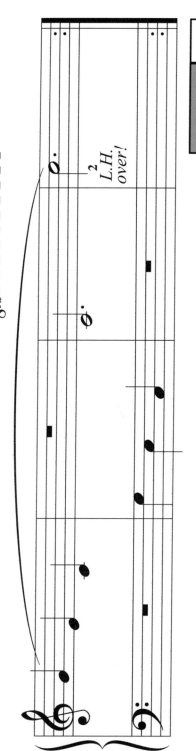

DID IT!

DAY TWO

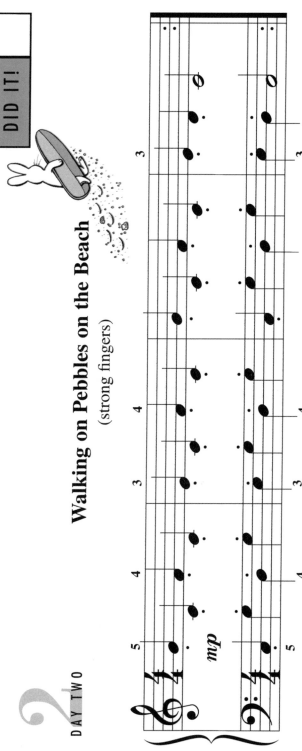

Walking on Pebbles on the Beach
(strong fingers)

DID IT!

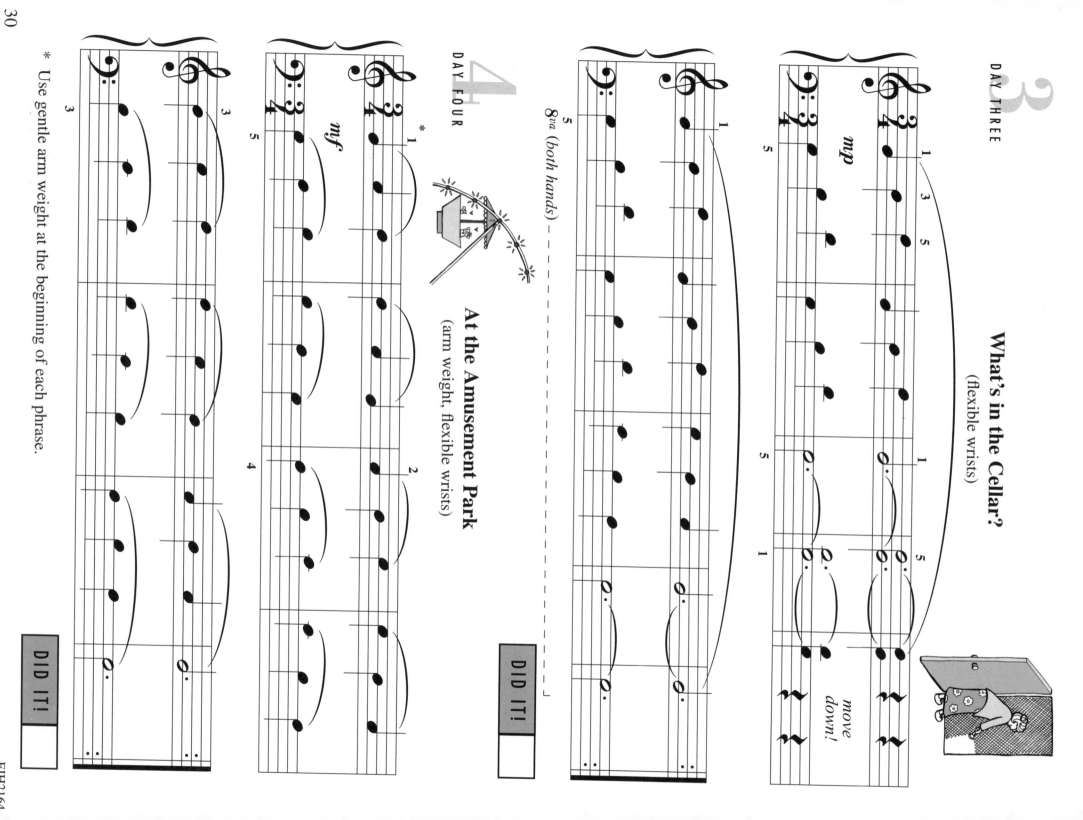

DAY THREE 3

What's in the Cellar?
(flexible wrists)

mp

move down!

8va (both hands)

DID IT!

DAY FOUR 4

At the Amusement Park
(arm weight, flexible wrists)

mf

DID IT!

* Use gentle arm weight at the beginning of each phrase.

DAY FIVE

Orange Popsicles
(arm weight, flexible wrists)

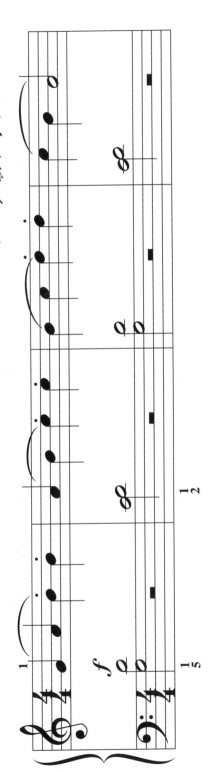

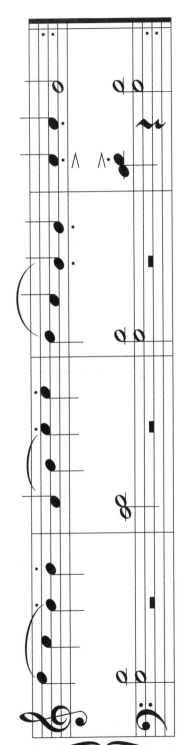

DID IT!

 LESSON DAY

- Play your favorite piece of the week for your teacher. Then, your teacher may have you play another one.

Teacher comments: _____

Certificate of Achievement

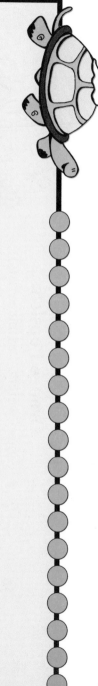

_____

has successfully completed

ENERGIZE YOUR FINGERS™
EVERY DAY
BOOK 1

of The FJH Pianist's Curriculum®

You are now ready for **Book 2A**

_____

Date

_____

Teacher's Signature